T0380912

VISION JOURNAL

A New Way to Do a Vision Board

Latifahia Brown

Scriptures taken from the Holy Bible, New International Version®, NIV®. Copyright © 1973, 1978, 1984, 2011 by Biblica, Inc.™ Used by permission of Zondervan. All rights reserved worldwide. www.zondervan.com The "NIV" and "New International Version" are trademarks registered in the United States Patent and Trademark Office by Biblica, Inc.

WestBow Press books may be ordered through booksellers or by contacting:

WestBow Press
A Division of Thomas Nelson & Zondervan
1663 Liberty Drive
Bloomington, IN 47403
www.westbowpress.com
1 (866) 928-1240

ISBN: 978-1-9736-4845-1 (sc)
ISBN: 978-1-9736-4846-8 (e)

Library of Congress Control Number: 2018914847

Print information available on the last page.

WestBow Press rev. date: 01/11/2019

WESTBOW
PRESS®
A DIVISION OF THOMAS NELSON
& ZONDERVAN

This Vision Journal Belongs to:

_____

Date:

_____

Topics Addressed

[Introduction]

This Vision Journal is not your typical Vision Board. Most times when Vision Boards are done, they are done with poster boards and what you desire. But I want you to reevaluate or modify your thinking about how you think about creating a Vision Board.

A lot of times we think, as Christians, about the things we desire, but tend to forsake what the Lord desires for us. In this Vision Journal, I challenge you as you construct each page, to consider what the Lord would desire for you to have in health, finance, family, career, ministry, etc.

Ask: How will the Lord want to use me in this area of my life?

Remember this life is not about just us, but how we can glorify the Lord in every aspect of our lives.

"Trust in the Lord and do good; dwell in the land and enjoy safe pasture. Take delight in the Lord, and he will give you the desires of your heart. Commit your way to the Lord; trust in him and he will do this:"

(Psalm 37: 4-5 NIV)

The Lord wants you to trust Him, commit to Him, do good, and He will give you the desires of your heart. You may had realized that sometimes the things we desire, may not be the plans He has for us. It's still ok to ask the Lord but be prepared for whatever He wants for you. I'm not saying that you must not think about yourself, but this life is beyond us. If you always desire things for selfishness, then you need to reevaluate your motives. It's ok to want, but just check your heart to why you want what you want. For example: Is it to say to people, "I have money." Or "Look at me, look at what I can afford." Rather than saying, "I want to make money, so I able to bless other people with it." Remember, the things that we are given are not ours, but a gift from the Lord.

It is great to think about what the Lord wants for you. If you are not sure about how the Lord wants to use in this life time, then pray and ask the Lord for guidance. Use this Vision Journal as a reminder of what you think the Lord wants to do in your life.

After completing each page or the book, pray:

Lord if this is in your will for this to happen, may Your will be done.

If this Vision Journal is a blessing to you, then please give a Vision Journal for those that you love, like your child (you are never too young to have a vision), a family member, a church member, or for a group of women that just need encouragement. It will truly bless them!

HAVE FUN CREATING!

How to Use the Vision Journal Book

- This Vision Journal Book is a Mixed Media Art book, so use any type of art tools to create the vision for each category. Gather materials that you will use to create your vision like scrapbook paper, magazines, scissors, glue, paint, markers, color pencils, etc. You can draw, paint, scrapbook, write, etc. Be as creative as you would like.

- Since there are many topics to address, please pace yourself through the workbook.

- Brainstorming papers are provided for you, so you can write down or draw your ideas.

- Remember this is your book and it would be great to look at it daily as a reminder of how the Lord is working in the different areas of your life.

- This book is perfect for:

    o Women's Groups

    o Youth Groups

    o Retreats

    o Church/Bible Studies

    o Family time

    o Bible Study Groups

Let's Create!!

Scripture(s)

What scriptures will encourage you from day to day as a reminder of God's love? These scriptures are great reminders when you are really going through and just need simple encouragement.

Relationship with Jesus

What would you like your relationship with Jesus to look like?

What can you do to make your relationship better with Christ?

Health/Self-Care

How would you want the Lord to intervene in your health?

What changes would you make to better your health?

Finances

How would you like the Lord to intervene in your finances?

What would you like your finances to look like?

Career

Where do you think the Lord wants you in your career?

What career do you desire?

How can you serve the Lord in your career?

Family

What do you feel the Lord desires for your spouse,
children, or other immediate family members?

How do you want to play a role in your family?

Ministry

It is always great to share your gifts with the Body of Christ, the Church. It is not just meant to keep for ourselves.

Remember ministry takes place in and out of the church, how would you like to share your gifts with the church?

Hobbies/Interests

What gives you joy that you wouldn't mind doing as a stress relief?

What new hobbies would you not mind trying?

What do you love doing that you have neglected, but you want to continue?

What Makes Your Heart Happy?

What are the small things that can make your day?

Example: Getting coffee, walking through Barnes N' Nobles, etc.

[Brainstorm Time!]

Use these papers to brainstorm ideas for your pages in your workbook.

Think About It!

*(Optional)- Please take this out and use it to brainstorm your ideas. *

Topic: _____

Your Desires (What are some realistic desires you have for this area of your life?)	The Lord's Desires (What do you think the Lord desires for you to do in this area of your life?)

*What can you do to reach these goals i.e. pray/read scripture/research programs?

*(Optional)- Use the back of this page to sketch or map out what you want on your pages. *

Think About It!

*(Optional)- Please take this out and use it to brainstorm your ideas. *

Topic: _____

Your Desires (What are some realistic desires you have for this area of your life?)	The Lord's Desires (What do you think the Lord desires for you to do in this area of your life?)

*What can you do to reach these goals i.e. pray/read scripture/research programs?

*(Optional)- Use the back of this page to sketch or map out what you want on your pages. *

Think About It!

*(Optional)- Please take this out and use it to brainstorm your ideas. *

Topic: _____

Your Desires (What are some realistic desires you have for this area of your life?)	The Lord's Desires (What do you think the Lord desires for you to do in this area of your life?)

*What can you do to reach these goals i.e. pray/read scripture/research programs?

*(Optional)- Use the back of this page to sketch or
map out what you want on your pages. *

Think About It!

*(Optional)- Please take this out and use it to brainstorm your ideas. *

Topic: _____

Your Desires (What are some realistic desires you have for this area of your life?)	The Lord's Desires (What do you think the Lord desires for you to do in this area of your life?)

*What can you do to reach these goals i.e. pray/read scripture/research programs?

*(Optional)- Use the back of this page to sketch or map out what you want on your pages. *

Think About It!

Topic: _____

Your Desires (What are some realistic desires you have for this area of your life?)	The Lord's Desires (What do you think the Lord desires for you to do in this area of your life?)

*What can you do to reach these goals i.e. pray/read scripture/research programs?

*(Optional)- Use the back of this page to sketch or
map out what you want on your pages. *

Think About It!

*(Optional)- Please take this out and use it to brainstorm your ideas. *

Topic: _____

<u>Your Desires</u> (What are some realistic desires you have for this area of your life?)	<u>The Lord's Desires</u> (What do you think the Lord desires for you to do in this area of your life?)

*What can you do to reach these goals i.e. pray/read scripture/research programs?

*(Optional)- Use the back of this page to sketch or map out what you want on your pages. *

Think About It!

*(Optional)- Please take this out and use it to brainstorm your ideas. *

Topic: _____

Your Desires (What are some realistic desires you have for this area of your life?)	The Lord's Desires (What do you think the Lord desires for you to do in this area of your life?)

*What can you do to reach these goals i.e. pray/read scripture/research programs?

*(Optional)- Use the back of this page to sketch or
map out what you want on your pages. *

Think About It!

*(Optional)- Please take this out and use it to brainstorm your ideas. *

Topic: _____

Your Desires (What are some realistic desires you have for this area of your life?)	The Lord's Desires (What do you think the Lord desires for you to do in this area of your life?)

*What can you do to reach these goals i.e. pray/read scripture/research programs?

*(Optional)- Use the back of this page to sketch or map out what you want on your pages. *

Think About It!

*(Optional)- Please take this out and use it to brainstorm your ideas. *

Topic: _____

Your Desires (What are some realistic desires you have for this area of your life?)	The Lord's Desires (What do you think the Lord desires for you to do in this area of your life?)

*What can you do to reach these goals i.e. pray/read scripture/research programs?

*(Optional)- Use the back of this page to sketch or
map out what you want on your pages. *

Think About It!

*(Optional)- Please take this out and use it to brainstorm your ideas. *

Topic: _____

Your Desires (What are some realistic desires you have for this area of your life?)	The Lord's Desires (What do you think the Lord desires for you to do in this area of your life?)

*What can you do to reach these goals i.e. pray/read scripture/research programs?

*(Optional)- Use the back of this page to sketch or
map out what you want on your pages. *

[**Next Steps**]

(Let's go beyond just your desires! Let's take action!)

[Goals]

What are some immediate and reasonable goals that you can start to initiate now? The Lord has given us tools to help us reach our goals/desires. How do you utilize those tools?

Use a planner or organizer to help you set your goals as well. As you set your goal, pray that the Lord's Will be done and that the Lord would give you strength to meet that goal.

Example: I will research a financial education class like Dave Ramsey to initiate my goal to get out of debt.

_____

☐   Goal 1:

☐   Start Date:

☐   Date Accomplished:

_____

☐   Goal 2:

☐   Start Date:

☐   Date Accomplished:

_____

☐   Goal 3:

☐   Start Date:

☐   Date Accomplished:

_____

☐   Goal 4:

☐   Start Date:

☐   Date Accomplished:

□ Goal 5:

□ Start Date:
□ Date Accomplished:

□ Goal 6:

□ Start Date:
□ Date Accomplished:

□ Goal 7:

□ Start Date:
□ Date Accomplished:

□ Goal 8:

□ Start Date:
□ Date Accomplished:

□ Goal 9:

□ Start Date:
□ Date Accomplished:

⌈ **Accountability** ⌉

Now that you have a few goals set. Now it's time for you to select someone that will hold you accountable to reach your goals. We were not intended to walk this life alone. We were meant to desire companionship/fellowship.

I challenge you to pick someone you trust to hold you accountable to your goals/desires. That can be a best friend, a church member, a pastor, a family member, etc. They will be the person that can help pray and push you to reach your goal.

Name of my accountability partner: _____

Reflection

Throughout the year, take the time to reflect on how the Lord has answered your prayers/ desires you had in this book. It always helps to reflect, so you can see what the Lord is doing in your life. Write it down below or on the Vision Journal Workbook page(s).

Resources

The Lord has given us many tools and here are a couple of tools that I found helpful in my personal growth. Here are a few resources:

Spiritual Encouragement:

- The Bible or a Study Bible
- "Battlefield of the Mind" by Joyce Meyers
- Any books by Joyce Meyers, Priscilla Shirers, or other Christian authors
- Illustrated Bible (www.dayspring.com)
- Listen to sermons online by Joyce Meyers (www.joycemeyer.org), Priscilla Shirer, or listen to your favorite pastor/speaker/teacher
- Small groups/Bible Studies

Fitness:

- Gym
- Personal Trainer
- Beachbody (Home fitness and nutrition)

Finances:

- Dave Ramsey's Financial Peace University (there are online tools that you can use)
- Prime America
- Accountant

Organizational Tools for House, Schedule, or Goals:

- "The Simplified Life" by Emily Ley
- "The Simplified Planner" by Emily Ley
- Planners by Erin Condren
- Cultivate What Matters (www.cultivatewhatmatters.com)

Cute Stickers to Use for Your Vision Journal/Setting Goals/Planners:

- Cultivate What Matters (www.cultivatewhatmatters.com)
- Illustrated Faith Stickers (Michaels Store, www.dayspring.com)

About Olivia Madison Gifts

I, Latifahia Brown, started Olivia Madison Gifts because I wanted to give my daughter, Olivia Madison, who has Down Syndrome, the opportunity to learn skills, so she can join me in the business in the future. In my shop you will find gifts that help encourage others like: Vision Journals, Spiritual Growth Journals, spa gifts (sugar scrubs, rice heat/cold pads, linens sprays), stationery (invitations, personalized stationery, and mini slide out gift cards/thank you cards), and pillows.

Follow my journey with Olivia at: www.ltausp15.wixsite.com/blog
Shop at: www.etsy.com/shop/oliviamadisongifts
Join us for the Vision Journal Challenge on Facebook.
If this Vision Journal was a blessing to you, then bless someone else with one. You can find them at my shop.

[About the Author]

Latifahia Brown is an Educator for over 11 years, a Stay at Home Working Mom, a Wife, a Mom of 3, and a Small Business Owner (Olivia Madison Gifts). Most of all she loves Jesus! Latifahia's passion in life is to: 1) live for Christ and 2) to encourage people to take care of the 1 body the Lord has given them- spiritually, physically, emotionally, and mentally.

After having her 3rd child and transitioning in her career, she became very overwhelmed with life and she found herself stuck. With Latifahia creating content in the classroom, she decided to create content, The Vision Journal Workbook, for herself/others, where she could use an artistic outlet to get a better vision on the life the Lord had for her. This workbook is for: 1) people that are stuck with the overwhelming feeling of life, 2) for people that just want clear direction in their lives, and 3) people that want to reestablish their relationship with Christ. May this book be a blessing to you and others!